May this be a gift that brings you peace and comfort.

With warm regards,

[signature] MSW, CRM

Until Death Do Us Part
A Letter To Our Loved Ones

By Yvonne C. Ametller Dunetz, MSW, Reiki Master
Photographs by Al Pollakusky

AUTHOR: Yvonne C. Ametller Dunetz, MSW

PHOTOGRAPHY: Al Pollakusky

COVER DESIGN: Lopa Shroff

COVER PHOTOGRAPH: Yvonne C. Ametller Dunetz

LAYOUT : H. Donald Kroitzsh

Almond Tree Press is a registered Trademark of YCD Professional Management Consultants, Inc.

Published by:
Almond Tree Press
P.O. Box 3327
Nashua, New Hampshire 03061-3327
Website: www.almondtreepress.com

Prepared by:
Five Corners Press
Plymouth, Vermont 05056

Printed and bound in the United States of America

ISBN: 0-9768914-0-9   US$21.⁹⁵

Acknowledgements

This book and CD, *Until Death Do Us Part, A Letter To Our Loved Ones*, was part of another book that I have been writing, that will be completed by the summer of 2005. I knew in my heart, that this part of my original work needed to be separate. Although the book is small, its message is powerful and needed to stand alone.

Since I have been a little girl, I have always known that people come in and out of our lives at different times for a reason. I have been very blessed. I have gone through my life with tremendous faith knowing that we each have a purpose in life, that life is short and that we are each here for a reason. I am a very spiritual person that has been guided in a very profound way. I have not been alone in my work or in my life. I am very thankful and grateful for all of my blessings.

Understanding that it is our relationships that have the most profound meaning in our lives, I would like to acknowledge the following people who have been very supportive of this work: My sister, Vivienne Pollakusky. Thank you for being there for me. Al Pollakusky, thank you for the beautiful photographs and for understanding what I was trying to achieve. Michaeline Della Fera, thank you for sharing your knowledge as an author and for providing me with a wealth of information and support. You have been so gracious and kind to me. Dorothy Elizabeth Sarette, thank you for introducing me to Charles and for your positive presence when the CD was being recorded. Charles Parenteau, thank you for generously sharing your time and musical talents. And thank you for recognizing the importance of this project. Beth Parenteau, thank you for sharing Charles with me. Carol Renwick, thank you for understanding ancient geometry and for being a kindred spirit. Carolyn Choate and Gordon Jackson, thank you for your expertise and enthusiasm. Latha and Krishna Mangipudi, thank you for your unwavering support and for Krishna being such a great computer guru. Don Kroitzsh and Lopa Shroff, thank you for helping to make this project come to life. To my loved ones, my family and my friends, thank you for being a special part of my life. You shall always be very dear to me.

Dedication

This book is dedicated to all of our Loved Ones, those who have passed over to the other side and those who are still with us.

Until Death Do Us Part

I think that if our loved ones could come back and communicate with us or leave us a letter...

I believe that this is what they would say:

My Dear Loved Ones;

If I left you suddenly without a chance to say good-bye

*If we did not have the time to share some last minute thoughts and
    feelings*

If there were questions still unanswered
*Or pain that occurred within our relationship that we had yet to resolve
    and heal*

If I had been very sick and you were by my side
If I had been so distraught and my will to live was no longer

If there were still so many dreams that we had yet to realize together

I would want you to remember this…
You mean the world to me.

My life has been enriched by being a part of yours.
The time that we had to share with one another was precious.
We grew together, we loved together, and we experienced life together.

How fortunate we are to have had each other in our lives.

Please forgive me for any pain that I have caused you.

Please forgive me for my lack of foresight or understanding that which I did not comprehend was important to you.

Please forgive me if I had not been there for you when you needed me.

Please forgive me for any unkind words we may have expressed.

Please forgive me for my imperfections.

Please forgive me for not having had the chance to tell you so many things that I had wanted to express.

Please forgive me for leaving you at this time of our lives.

Please forgive me for leaving you so unexpectedly.

Please do not be angry with me.

Thank you for all that we have shared together.
Thank you for your friendship.
Thank you for your love and kindness.

Thank you for being there for me.
Thank you for knowing just what to do and say.
Thank you for trying to figure out what to do or what to say when you
did not know.

Thank you for your hugs and kisses.
Thank you for wiping away my tears.
Thank you for giving me encouragement and hope.

Thank you for believing in me.

Thank you for all the times you have comforted me.

Thank you for your tender loving care.

Thank you for sharing your life's experiences with me.

Please remember that my love for you is something I will cherish forever.

We are a part of each other that goes beyond space and time.

Our love is what gave us strength and courage while I was alive.

Our love is what will continue to give you strength and courage to live your life to its fullest until we meet again.

*Please know that although I am not physically with you,
I am with you always.*

My love is with you always.

As you live each day of your life
As you fulfill your purpose

As you celebrate each birthday, wedding, happy and sad occasions of
    your lives
Remember, I am with you in spirit.

Light a candle to remember me.
Plant a tree in my honor.

Feel my presence always with you reminding you that you are never
  alone and that
My love is with you forever.

My Dear Loved Ones…

*Thank you for your friendship, for your love, and for being part of my
life. I hope that my life has enriched yours as much as you have
enriched mine.*

Please remember and know that we will always be a part of each other.

I love you dearly.

My thoughts, my prayers, and my love are with you always.